Quiet Leadership

By Julian Stodd

QUIET LEADERSHIP

Copyright © 2021 by Julian Stodd

All rights reserved. This book, or any portion thereof may not be reproduced or used in any manner whatsoever without the express written permission of the publisher except for the use of brief quotations in a book review.

ISBN - Paperback 978-1-8380196-2-4 | eBook 978-1-8380196-3-1

Sea Salt Publishing
Bournemouth, Dorset, UK

Websites:

www.seasaltlearning.com

www.julianstodd.wordpress.com

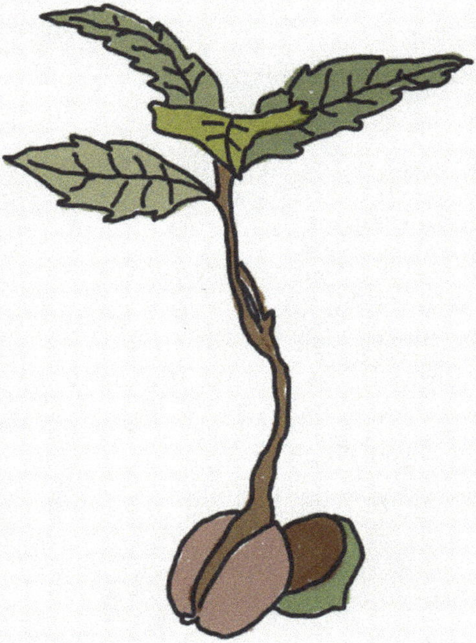

CONTENTS

QUIET LEADERSHIP — 6
- Introduction — 6
- The Four Seasons of Quiet Leadership — 8
- The Organisation As Ecosystem — 10
- 'Every day, through my small actions…' — 12
- Nobody Alone — 13
- The Story So Far — 15
- How to use this Book — 16
- The Quiet Leadership Research Project — 18

HUMILITY — 21
- Humility — 22
- Reflection - Shadow - Impact — 24
- Intention - Action - Impact — 26
- Quiet Leadership Questions — 28
- Question 1: What shadow do you cast? — 29
- Things That We Give - Things That We Take Away — 30
- Every Day — 32
- Question 2: What is your Hope? — 35
- What Our Research Says About Humility — 36

KINDNESS — 39
- Kindness — 40
- Battered by the Storms — 42
- Friction on the System — 44
- Question 3: Why does Kindness count? — 46
- Intent or Impact? — 47
- Where are we kindest? — 48
- Question 4: Growing with Kindness — 50
- Every Action — 51
- What Our Research Says about Kindness — 52

FAIRNESS — 55
- As We Find Strength — 56
- How Do We Experience Fairness? — 58
- Question 5: With Fairness, Where Does Our Responsibility Lie? — 62
- How Fairness is Split — 64
- Question 6: Does Your Power Promote Growth? — 67
- Reaching Down — 68
- Leaving with Less #1 — 71
- What Our Research Says About Fairness — 72

GRACE — 75
- The Breeze — 76
- Weathering The Winter Storms — 78
- The Forest Grows from the Floor — 79
- An Endless Weight — 80
- Question 7: What Weight Do You Carry? — 81
- To Leave With Less #2 — 82
- Question 8: What Can You Leave Behind — 83
- What Our Research Says About Grace — 84

QUIET LEADERSHIP IN PRACTICE — 86
- Quiet Leadership — 88
- Walking Through The Forest — 90

FURTHER READING — 92

INTRODUCTION

When Organisations talk about leadership, they mark out a journey that is 10,000 steps long. Quiet Leadership is about the first three steps.

It's an exploration of leadership in the smallest of things: our mindset, our words and our actions, in every single day.

It's not about a grand aspiration, about formal objectives, or big development programmes.

It's not about the formal power you have been given, your ability to influence at scale, or the varied ways you exert control.

It's not about 'one' way of leading, but rather about a multitude of ways, and specifically about how you find 'your' way.

Quiet Leadership is about the ways we are with each other in every moment, and how those varied 'ways' of being come together to give us the thing we call culture today.

It's a practice that recognises that all cultures have edges, all communities have boundaries, and our impact is felt more in the shadows than in the light that we face.

Quiet Leadership is a reflective practice, not to see the version of ourselves that we already know, but, rather, to discover ourselves in how others see us.

Leadership in our reflection; leadership in our shadow. Leadership in our impact, through every action every day.

QUIET LEADERSHIP

THE FOUR SEASONS OF QUIET LEADERSHIP

As this work has taken shape, I have phrased it in terms of the four seasons of every year, representing four central ideas: 'Humility', 'Kindness', 'Fairness', and 'Grace'.

In the Winter, we will start with the acorn—the potential of our leadership—and look inside for the leader that we wish to be.

We will consider **Humility**, to understand the extent to which it is held in our intention, our action or our impact.

As the first green shoots poke out through the snow, as we cast our first shadow in the weak winter light, we consider the ways we are experienced by others as a leader, from the very start of our journey.

In the Springtime, we will look at the **Kindness** with which we grow. As we gain power and status, we impact others within the system, but do we do so equally, and do we recognise the ways we cause friction as we grow?

Humility
In Our Mindset

Kindness
In Our Approach

The Summer sees the tree reach maturity. As our canopy spreads, as we find a magnificent strength and power, we will look at Kindness. We will ask ourselves how we use our power: to serve ourselves, or to shelter others?

Finally, come the Autumn, we must shed our leaves, we must decide what we can leave behind before we face the winter ahead. If a tree carries every leaf into the winter storms, the weight of the snow will break its branches. This is the notion of **Grace**: a fluidity of action.

We must choose the loss that we will experience because we cannot carry everything forward; Leadership as a practice of growth, maturity, loss and renewal.

Quiet Leadership is leadership through the smallest of actions, in each and every day.

Fairness
In Our Actions

Grace
In Letting Go

THE ORGANISATION AS ECOSYSTEM

Consider the Organisation that you work for as an ecosystem: a landscape that stretches out in front of you.

Some parts of it are familiar—those that are local to you, or that you visit often.

Other parts are foreign, distant, or lie as wilderness.

Each of us can look after one area. You may tend to a field, I can care for a tree in the forest, someone else stands on the riverbank and clears the litter from the path.

Through our individual action, we make our own part better, and yet, the ecosystem as a whole may not thrive.

Some parts flourish, others are denuded, some are simply out of sight and mind.

No one of us can care for the whole landscape, and yet, the way we treat the ecosystem affects us all.

We are interconnected: my actions have an effect, not simply in front of me, in full sight, but in the ways that they interact, cascade through to, or influence, others.

If I behave in certain ways, I give others permission or space to do so too.

If I 'take' from the system, I demonstrate that 'taking' is acceptable.

If I push, then others push back.

Much of this takes place in our 'everyday'—not through grand ideas and large-scale initiatives, but through our action in the moment.

We impact our ecosystem in the smallest of ways, and yet, those small ways, combined, change everything.

If the water is polluted, the skies fill with fumes or the wells are run dry, we all suffer.

Quiet Leadership takes this ecosystem view. It says that the system can only be healthy, our Organisation can only thrive, if we are connected and if we care.

And yet, it also recognises that we cannot impose this state. No one of us alone can save us all.

No one of us alone can tend to the whole forest or plain.

On this journey into Quiet Leadership, we will explore how we can tend to the ecosystem together: beyond hierarchy, beyond what is local, beyond what is mine.

Through the smallest of actions, we can change everything, if everyone takes the smallest of actions.

Quiet Leadership looks at how we do this—how we care for our ecosystem so that we can thrive within it.

'EVERY DAY, THROUGH MY SMALL ACTIONS...'

The central notion to hold onto is that we all enhance our ecosystem, and we all degrade it.

If it were as simple as all of us 'wishing' that things were better, then the problem would already be solved. But it isn't.

In fact, it's worse: The challenges of culture persist, despite all of us thinking like this.

Because thinking is not enough.

Culture is an asset created and recreated in the moment. It's an aggregation of behaviour, not a reflection of intent. It's a group social phenomenon.

Every day, through my small actions, and the ways that those actions land in the shadows, our culture is formed.

The Organisation As Ecosystem
© Julian Stodd

Every Day Through Small Actions

We Enhance AND Degrade

The System Around Us

NOBODY ALONE

If no one of us alone can tend to the whole ecosystem, then how is the system kept healthy?

Quiet Leadership considers the ecosystem interconnected, through webs that are largely invisible to their fullest extent. Whilst our individual action cannot change the system by force, that action is nonetheless observed at a local level.

The way that we are, the ways that we act, the things that we say and the behaviours we exhibit all land within the landscape.

Each of these things does one of two things: It makes the system better, or it degrades it.

It is a leaf that lands on the forest floor, or a piece of rubbish lodged in the hedgerow.

When we take these smallest of actions, and make the system better, we do not do so simply for ourselves; we create a space for others to gather around.

Our actions help to create a culture that, overall, impacts the ecosystem at scale. If we make our garden, our field, our part of the forest better, then others may move in the same direction, as we create a narrative, a norm, a space for behaviour to flourish.

If only it were this simple. The litter of our cultural landscape, the refuse strewn through our organisational ecosystem, is not like the rubbish thrown from a moving car. Much of it is neither deliberately cast aside, nor does it visibly represent rubbish.

The degradation of our ecosystem does not often occur through bad people doing bad things; rather, it occurs because of good people, like you and me, doing good but disconnected things, or simply because we do nothing. We look away, or we fail to see what falls in our shadow.

As we explore Quiet Leadership, we will come back, time and again, to our shadow. It's the mechanism by which we end up fragmented, separate, in a forest that is dying, polluted not by intent but by inaction, not by bad people but by the impact of all people.

THE STORY SO FAR

If no one of us alone can tend to the whole ecosystem, then how is the system kept healthy?

Let's draw together the story so far. We can view the Organisation that we work for as an ecosystem, with every part connected. Each day, we take something from and contribute to the system. And yet, the system cannot be healthy through the actions of one person alone.

We are interconnected.

As we explore Quiet Leadership, we will seek to tease this apart:

- We will start with Humility, to consider our reflection, shadow, and impact.
- We will move on to Kindness, to discover the social currencies, and the ways we create friction within the system.
- We will discover Fairness, and ask whether we use our power to promote growth.
- Finally we will consider how we lead with Grace: to constantly adapt our course and let things go

HOW TO USE THIS BOOK

This book is set up to guide you through the landscape of Quiet Leadership: I cannot make the journey for you, but I hope I can help you to find your way across.

As we travel, we may each see the same landmarks—the same mountains in the distance, the same forests and valley floor, the same rivers and hills. We will travel through the four seasons.

But each of us will put our foot down in a different place; each of us, at the end of the journey, will carry different mud on their boots. And the understanding of Quiet Leadership is about the mud that you pick up.

Whilst we may all make it back to the start, the journey we make is unique to each of us.

This book is structured into four main sections, each one covering one of the four seasons of Quiet Leadership: Humility, Kindness, Fairness, and Grace.

Whilst I would encourage you to explore these in order, there is no need to do so.

For each area, I will try to create a space to explore, through sharing what the research tells us, asking questions and giving you my perspective.

You can make this journey alone, but you could just as well take it with others.

Across the four sections, there are eight questions in total, which you can use as the basis of a conversation. If you are making this journey with someone else, I would encourage you to take at least half an hour with each question.

Alternatively, I regularly guide open groups through this Landscape, and you would be welcome to join me in doing so. Just check on the website for when our next open journey will be.

Remember: You are not accountable to anyone for the journey that you make, nor are you limited to only travelling through this landscape once.

As I pull this body of work together, some of it represents a second, or even a third attempt to explore this space. My earliest 'framework for fairness' and work on 'Social Leadership Leaves' evolved into 'Why Kindness Counts', and now into 'Quiet Leadership'.

Is this the end of that journey?

I do not know, but I doubt it. When we come to our final section on Grace, I will talk about a fluidity of thinking and action—a willingness to interpret things anew, to leave something behind and to constantly correct our course and action. And that is what we should all practice in our Leadership.

For now, I view Quiet Leadership as the right journey to make, and I look forward to travelling this landscape with you.

Quiet Leadership

© Julian Stodd

Research Project

Julian Stodd

Accompanying this work is a global research project, exploring each of the four central themes.

This is social research—qualitative, subjective, personal. It is not a quest to find one 'answer' or to uncover one 'truth', but rather, to gather a richness of diverse experience.

For each of the core aspects of Humility, Kindness, Fairness and Grace, I am asking people to answer nine questions that explore their own understanding of these systems: what they are, why they are important, how they work and their experiences of the journey.

You are welcome to join in and contribute to this research. I will share some of the initial findings in this first edition of the Guidebook, but in time I hope to publish a larger book on the subject.

QUIET LEADERSHIP

HUMILITY
IN OUR MINDSET

HUMILITY

When I think about myself as a person, or a leader, I first look within, staring into the mirror, facing the light.

With a stark reality, I can see my smile, alongside a few wrinkles and some grey hair. Everything is clear to me.

But my impact is not held facing the light: often it is felt in my shadow.

Sometimes, my actions cause an effect that I can see—hopefully, a positive one for the people I know—but inevitably, my actions sometimes fall short, and I am aware of a negative outcome.

But positive effects and outcomes that I can see—these things take place in the light.

And yet, even in Organisations that are full of good people, people like you and me, bad effects occur. Effects in the darkness. People are lost in the cracks, or culture overall fails to be fair or effective.

How is this possible? If we are all looking into the light, why can't we see where the weakness is, or what needs to change? Why can't I simply turn around and see what needs to be done?

Because turning around is not enough.

When I turn, I still stand in the light. Instead of shining on my face, it lands on the back of my head and leaves me staring into the shadow. And still, I cannot see what I need to see.

And my impact is felt across both, in the light where I can see it, and in the shadow, into the dark.

Moreover, mine is not the only shadow.

Humility

Shadows
Culture

© Julian Stodd

We each cast a shadow, sometimes cast by different suns. Our shadows dance and play together, interlocking, getting darker.

With no intention to cause harm, we nonetheless, between us, within the ecosystem of our Organisations, create dark places.

We create spaces into which people slip, not because we are bad, but because we can only see in the light.

We all cast a shadow.

SEA SALT LEARNING 23

REFLECTION – SHADOW – IMPACT

Here's a framework for considering this:

Think about your Reflection, your Shadow, and your Impact.

Humility
To Look At Our

Reflection
Shadow
Impact

Your Reflection you can see when you look in the mirror.

This is your first dimension of Humility: to explore your reflection and see what you can observe or change in yourself, in the light.

Your Shadow lies behind you. The second dimension of Humility is to be consciously aware of your shadow. Where does your shadow fall?

Does it sit in spaces you know or in the spaces beyond?

Does it fall over the people you trust, like, respect, or to whom you are connected? Or does it fall beyond your networks?

Does it map against your areas of direct responsibility, or is it more nebulous than that?

Within your shadow lies your Impact.

Impact is not our intention but, rather, the effect of our action (or inaction).

But if your impact occurs in your shadow, how will you know how it lands?

How can you feel your impact?

To understand impact, we must look through the eyes of others. We need a community that can carry us into the dark spaces. In some ways, we need to earn the right to feel and hear it.

INTENTION – ACTION – IMPACT

Even in good systems, full of good people, bad outcomes occur. Partly, this is because we behave as a group, and partly, it's because our understanding of 'good' can be contextual, not absolute.

Gravity acts upon us all equally, but forces like 'fairness' do not. If you give me five dollars for a cake I have baked, I may consider that fair. If you give someone who is your friend ten dollars for a cake, they too may believe that you have acted fairly. But if I discover that you paid them twice as much, I may suddenly believe that what you did was unfair.

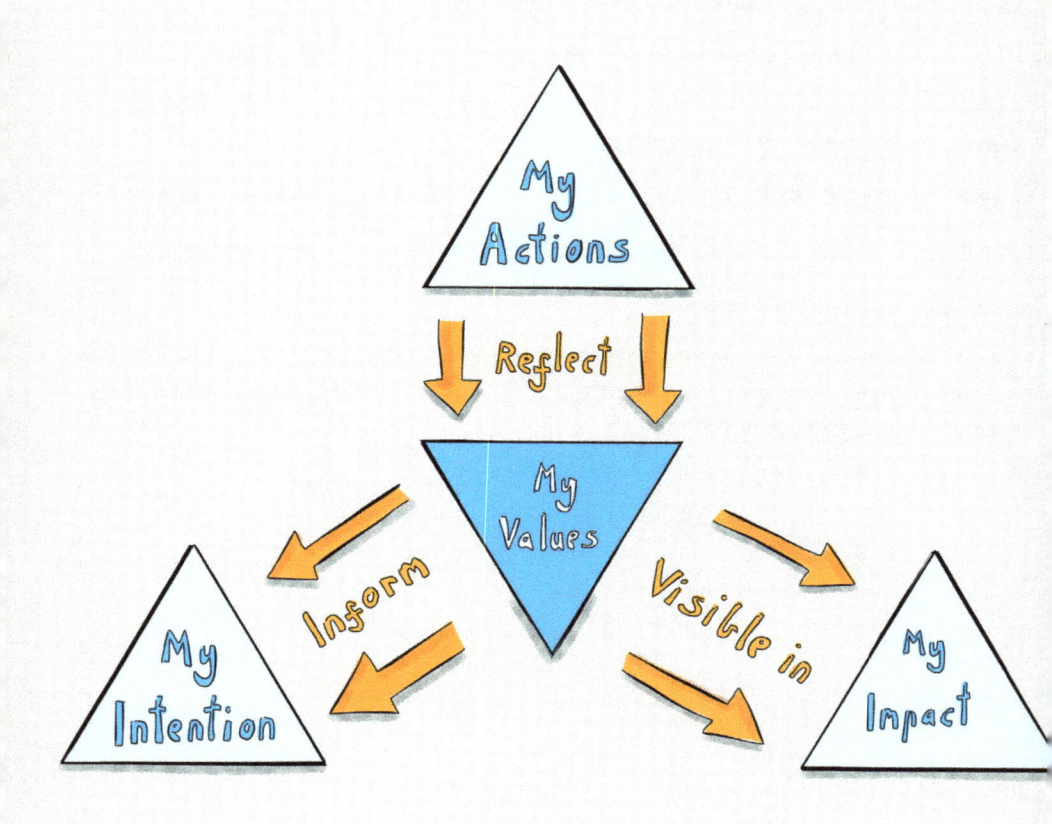

Our intention is held within us. It may guide our actions, but it does not determine them.

Our actions are carried out in the world; they may be shaped by our intentions but are not controlled by them, and they have an impact.

The impact of my actions is felt by different people in different ways. The impact may be a direct result of my action (i.e. my action causes it), but the outcome is not determined by my action (I may intend to act well, yet, the impact is bad).

Essentially, whilst I can control my intention and my actions, I cannot control or determine my impact.

But I have absolutely caused it.

This may seem rather abstract, but understanding where the cracks appear between intention, action and impact can help us to better understand why good people may still elicit bad outcomes, even if only when it lies out of their sight.

QUIET LEADERSHIP QUESTIONS

We have come to our first question. Throughout this journey, I will ask you to take time to consider eight of these questions in total.

You can do this in several ways:

- You may wish to simply sit and reflect (or, indeed, walk through the forest and reflect).
- You could choose to talk to someone you know, explain the context and invite them to discuss it over a coffee (virtual or otherwise).
- You could join one of the Quiet Leadership Open Cohorts and have this conversation with a stranger.

All of the questions that I ask you will be open to interpretation. When we are looking at Quiet Leadership, we are in a subjective landscape, and pretty much the only thing of which I can be sure is that you will read something new into it, different from what I have seen so far.

Humility

QUESTION 1:

What shadow do you cast?

What Shadow Do You Cast?

© Julian Stodd

You can interpret this question as you like, but remember to look beyond the obvious spaces.

SEA SALT LEARNING 29

THINGS THAT WE GIVE – THINGS THAT WE TAKE AWAY

I hope that you found value in your reflection on the shadow that you cast. There is no right answer to the question. Some people question the concept itself, whilst others find it a useful framework. Either way, it is the act of reflection within the context of our busy lives that is important.

If you wish to dig deeper into this aspect of Quiet Leadership, you may wish to address this supplementary question: What things do you give, and what do you take away?

The Organisation As Ecosystem
© Julian Stodd

Things That We Give

Things That We Take Away

I will share how I may interpret this for myself:

- I think that I give my thinking to my community by openly sharing my work and writing.
- I think that I give kindness to my community by remembering to say 'thank you' to people.
- I think that I share my uncertainty with my community, in the hope that others will feel that they can too.
- I think that I sometimes speak too much, or over people, which removes their voice and space—not because I intend to, but because I am excitable, but that is how our shadows are cast.
- I think that I give feedback badly and erratically, which creates an uncertain space for those with whom I work.
- I think that I claim a wide space in which to work, but perhaps by so doing, I use up more of the free air than I realise; my freedom may come at others' cost.

Of course, the question 'What do you take?' is a little like the question in an interview: 'What are your weaknesses?' (Is honesty and hard work a weakness?). Though we may pull our punches or even lie to ourselves, again, it is the act of reflection that counts. And as we have already said, 'reflection' is just one way to consider our humility.

EVERY DAY

Why bother to take small actions? If we cast a shadow, should we not simply deploy more lights and make them brighter?

Quiet Leadership may feel a bit like chipping away at a glacier with a toothpick. How can I possibly hope to influence or rebuild a culture when I have so much work to do on myself?

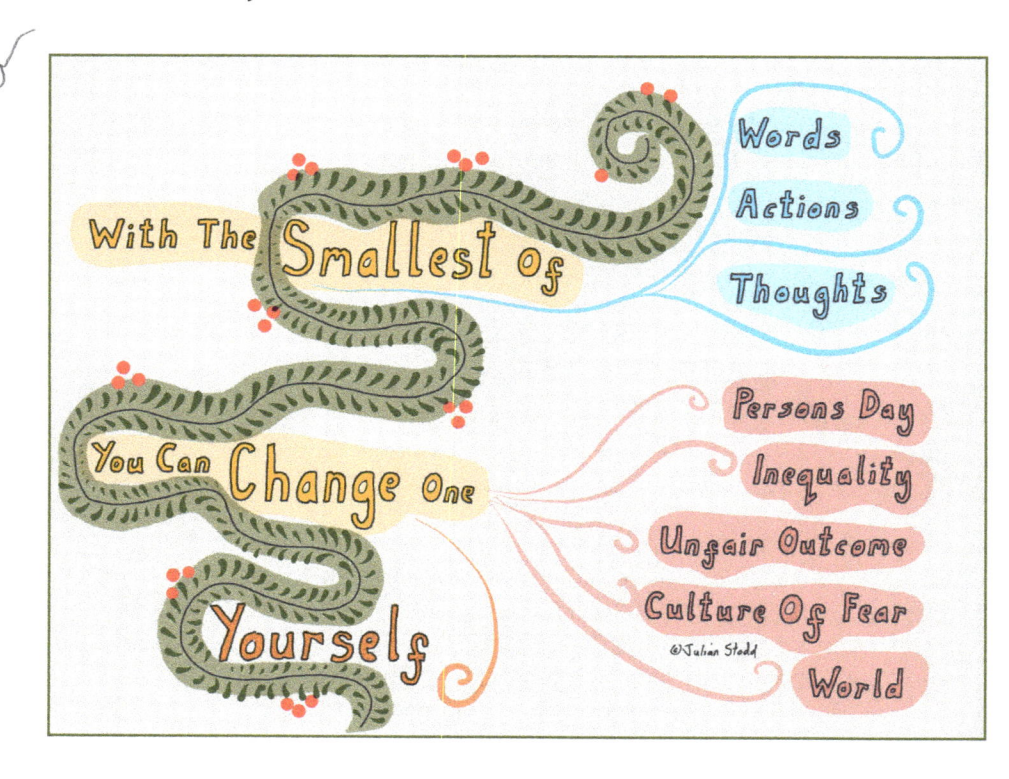

With The Smallest of Words, Actions, Thoughts You Can Change One Yourself, Persons Day, Inequality, Unfair Outcome, Culture Of Fear, World

©Julian Stodd

We can start with the smallest of . . . words. Words count. Words are powerful. Consider your use of words: how you use language, where you use words of condemnation or gratitude, vulnerability or fear. A single word can make a difference.

For example, I have been trying to avoid using the word 'guys' when I talk to my team. I always used to use this term to encapsulate everyone, but since reading Caroline Criado Perez's work on 'Invisible Women', I have realised that my language took something away. My language degraded the ecosystem. Changing it may only have a tiny effect, but it matters. It's not necessarily that my language alone polluted the system, but my language reinforced and perpetuated a dominant narrative that was invalid or outdated. So, through my action (using the word) and inaction (failing to change myself or challenge others), I degraded the system. I cast a shadow.

Words are good, but what about the smallest of actions? From picking up litter to washing a coffee cup, we make a difference. Perhaps the action you take is to reach out: to offer support, in kindness, to offer resource or challenge. Perhaps the action is to build or deconstruct. Perhaps it is to explore or debate, in search of new ideas or stories.

Even if you do not use small words or actions, you can still change something vital by taking time to think differently in the smallest of ways. By thinking differently, you can change yourself. Our fragments of thought create the 'meaning' and worldview within which we operate. Sometimes it is thought alone that fractures a framework and provides us with the space to truly grow.

With these thoughts, words and the smallest of actions, we can change many things.

- You can change one person's day, through the smallest of things.
- You can change one inequality, through a small action.
- You can change one unfair outcome, through your powerful small words or actions.
- You can challenge a culture of fear, through a powerful word or action.
- You can change the world, if your smallest of words captures the imagination, inspires or promotes others, knocks down a barrier or constraint, is shared with authentic power.

And, you never know. If you are willing to make a journey into Quiet Leadership, to consider the very smallest of your thoughts, your words and your actions, you may even change the hardest thing of all.

You may change yourself.

QUESTION 2:

What is your hope?

What Is Your Hope?

Again, you can interpret this question as you like:

- What is your hope for yourself as you become the leader that you wish to be?
- What is your hope for others as they seek to evolve themselves?
- What is your hope for your system—your organisation or society in general?
- What do you hope to achieve?
- What do you hope to leave behind?
- What shadow do you hope to throw back?
- What light do you hope to bring?

If we see Quiet Leadership as the acorn, with the first shoot breaking through, we seek balance: to understand the shadow and to understand the light.

WHAT OUR RESEARCH SAYS ABOUT HUMILITY

At first look, there is a strong belief that humility is a strength in leadership, but beyond that, we see variable beliefs. Overall, we see a lack of confidence in the language that people use to describe humility, which is typical of a subject about which we are uncertain. Respondents indicate that whilst humility is a strength, it is a difficult one to measure in others. Overall, we look for introspection, as well as a continuous sampling of feedback from others. There was a strong sense that humility is an active pursuit, that we must actively seek out other perspectives.

Below is a sample of the initial narrative ideas that we may read into 'Humility'.

- There is a strong belief that humility is a strength in leadership, but a weaker expectation that it makes a leader more effective.

- There is a wariness or lack of confidence in the language that people use to describe humility, which is typical of what we say when we are hesitant about our understanding. Answers also tended towards the central, or non-committal spaces.

- People indicate that they find it hard to determine whether a leader is humble, so we believe humility is a strength, but have some difficulty recognising it in leaders. We tend to lack confidence in our understanding.

- Key traits we associate with humility include thinking about others and the impact of our actions, a desire to hear what others say about us and, indeed, actively seeking out that information.

- There was a strong association between the words 'Curiosity' and 'Humility', expressed as the active searching to understand your impact in the system.

- A lot of descriptive phrases included 'self': self-reflection, self-analysis and the relationship of that 'self' to others. There is a dynamic nature in much of the language used.

- People talk about being self-aware and self-reflective in a given space, in a given context: What is my power and impact in this environment? In that sense, 'Humility' is viewed as a dynamic and active process.

Humility

QUIET LEADERSHIP

KINDNESS
IN OUR APPROACH

KINDNESS

We started with the acorn, our potential as a leader. Through the winter, we remained beneath the snow, until the first green shoot reached up for the light.

As we continue through the seasons of Quiet Leadership, we reach the Springtime: The seed lies behind us, and the sapling has emerged.

I have used the sapling as the metaphor for Kindness because the growth of the tree happens within the ecosystem, not abstracted from it.

As we grow, we are both nurtured and assailed by the atmospheric conditions that surround us.

Kindness is about growth, nurtured by the sun, battered by the storms.

Kindness

© Julian Stodd

SEA SALT LEARNING   41

BATTERED BY THE STORMS

But how are we battered?

Within Organisations, we are rarely touched by the weather itself, shielded by glass and air conditioning from the elements. Instead, we are battered by culture, by expectation, by convention, by ignorance, by complexity, by legacy, by opinion and by our existing knowledge.

Earlier, we considered our 'intention', our 'action' and our 'impact'. Whilst they are related, they are not determining.

My intention affects my actions, and my actions cause impact. But my intention does not determine what that impact will be.

As we grow, as we find power and position, as we learn and change, we are subject to expectation, peer pressure and review, the views and opinions of others, as well as our evolving expectations of ourselves.

In general, it seems likely that we all wish to be kind or, at the very least, to experience kindness in the actions of others.

A world where we had no expectation of kindness nor responsibility towards it would be a bleak one indeed.

And yet, kindness is not the universal state. Whilst we can spot bright lights in the landscape, they are not necessarily part of everyday experience, nor are they evenly distributed.

This is one of the themes that we will explore here. Do we lack kindness overall, or as we are battered by the wind and rain, does kindness become unevenly distributed and only accessible to some?

To me, this seems most likely. Only in rare instances do we deliberately set out to be unkind. But in many cases, the experience of kindness is uneven.

Through this part of our journey into Quiet Leadership, we will consider why.

FRICTION ON THE SYSTEM

It's easy to repeat what we already know, and we are all, without a doubt, experts in kindness.

Sometimes, there is value in reframing an idea or looking at it through a different lens.

Consider kindness in this way: What if it is friction that we exert on a system?

Friction?

Kindness is typically something we 'do', not simply what we think. And when we take action, we exert influence on the system that surrounds us. In the ecosystem approach, we are cutting down a tree or planting a crop.

Kindness touches other people, and when two things touch, we experience friction.

Friction generates heat and noise. When we hit the brakes on our car, the friction slows us down. But it is also friction that holds the tyres on the road. We need friction both to speed up and to slow down, to start and to stop.

In this sense, 'friction' is neither universally bad nor universally good, but it does impact other people.

Through our actions, we generate heat and noise into the system. And we do not touch everything or everyone equally.

Is Kindness The Friction We Exert Upon The System?

© Julian Stodd

QUESTION 3:

We talk about Kindness as though it were important. Use this, your third conversation, to explore why.

Why does Kindness count?

Why Does Kindness Count?

You can look at this from a variety of perspectives:

- Why does kindness count for me personally?
- Why is kindness important within an Organisation?
- More broadly, why is kindness important within society?

Equally, you could choose to explore it in the negative:

- What do we lose when kindness is absent?
- How do we experience or feel the lack or failure of kindness?
- Can we thrive without kindness?

INTENT OR IMPACT?

As our sapling grows in the Springtime showers and sun, we must ask ourselves a question: Is Kindness about the intent or the impact?

Is it enough for us to intend to be kind, or must our action be perceived as kindness for it to count?

Depending upon your view, one could see the following potential situations occurring:

Someone may believe that they are kind and act with what they believe is kindness, yet, be perceived as unkind.

Someone may make no effort to be kind, yet, be perceived as kind, judged by the way that they land in their system.

Someone may seek a bad outcome but achieve a good one, or seek a good one, yet, achieve nothing at all.

Or perhaps both must be true: Do we have to INTEND to be kind and be JUDGED as kind for Kindness to truly be present?

We will return to this thought again and again when we consider Humility and look forward to Fairness. Indeed, our understanding of this core tenet may be at the heart of Quiet Leadership in practice.

To what extent is our success in the judgement or the intent alone?

I have described Quiet Leadership as leadership in the smallest of actions, although I have also said that a thought can count. This is an unresolved question; perhaps this is the question for each of us to consider. Will your leadership be reflective alone, or reflective with action and iteration?

WHERE ARE WE KINDEST?

If we stand together in the Board Room, and it floods, then all our feet get equally wet. The floodwaters rise to a constant level. Kindness may not flood like that.

Ask yourself where you are kinder, with the people you know, the people you like or even the people you need?

It makes sense if the answer is, at least to some extent, 'yes'! After all, kindness is one of the Social Currencies, and these currencies are spent within our social structures.

It's not that I am not kind to strangers; rather, it's just that I am more likely to be kind to the people I know because kindness is one of the forces that bind us together.

Where I am kind to strangers, it may not be evenly distributed. I may tend to be more kind to people who are kind of like me: People who feel close by, or at the very least do not feel threatening or too different.

The notion that Kindness may not flow evenly around a system should not come as any surprise. Whilst Organisations may talk about values like 'fairness' and 'kindness' as ones that should permeate every part of the Organisation evenly, in reality, very few things are evenly distributed.

We hear talk of echo chambers—an uneven distribution of new knowledge.

We talk about inequality and gender-based inequity—an uneven distribution of power, wealth and opportunity.

We talk about opportunity, but it is often more readily available to those who already have at least some of it.

Social systems are inherently unequal because they are inherently divided into notions of 'us' and 'them'.

Even if not in conflict, we are connected in subsets of a whole.

Forces, such as Trust and Gratitude, often flow within these same uneven structures; indeed, forces of Trust may partly cause this unevenness.

Therefore, an act of Quiet Leadership may be to recognise the landscape, to recognise that even if we have got it right, in terms of our behaviours of kindness, we should ask ourselves if we have the distribution correct.

Or are people caught in the shadows where no kindness falls?

QUESTION 4:

How can you grow with Kindness in every day?

How Can You Grow With Kindness In Every Day?

©Julian Stodd

What I want you to explore here is somewhat practical in nature: Can we grow with Kindness, or indeed, SHOULD we seek to grow with Kindness every day?

If Kindness is something that we reserve for times when we have plenty, times of surplus, then it feels like a special occasion, not a culture or a practice.

But to be kind every day may feel artificial, inauthentic or even a burden. What about those days when you are exhausted or have nothing to give?

I guess this will relate back to the ways that we are kind: through thoughts, words, and actions.

When you stand in a field, on the edge of the forest, within our ecosystem, you feel the wind against your skin, but it is rarely a constant force.

Sometimes it blows hard; at other times, it dies away to a whisper. Perhaps that is how we grow with Kindness: at times with a whisper and at times with a shout.

Use your time in conversation to explore this: What 'feels' right, how would we know it is right, and how would we experience this in practice?

EVERY ACTION

We are drawing to the end of this season. Our acorn grew into a sapling; as it reaches up for the light, we have considered the ways that the young leaves are buffeted by the winds.

In the smallest of ways, the actions of every individual contribute to this effect. We hold intent, and we have impact, and the two may only have a tentative connection.

We each enhance and degrade the system, exerting friction upon it as we travel.

Our Quiet Leadership may lie in being mindful of this and looking towards the shadows, into our own shadow.

WHAT OUR RESEARCH SAYS ABOUT KINDNESS

Here are some snapshots from the initial research:

- People report variability in how they legislate their Kindness. They believe that they are kinder to people whom they know or need the most.

- This reinforces a view that Kindness plays a core role in bonding our social structures.

- There is strong agreement that Kindness matters, and it is more important to be kind than to take action at any cost.

- There is a rather even distribution as to whether Kindness is held primarily within the intent, or in our impact, but there is a stronger consistency of opinion that Kindness is a judgement, awarded mainly by others.

- This may indicate our unwillingness to accept that Kindness can be held in intent alone, the only thing that is actually under our direct scrutiny and control.

- Potentially, we could interpret that we don't have confidence in ourselves as the primary or solitary judge of Kindness.

- People were more comfortable describing Kindness than Humility. They used more formal, more analytical language, with greater fluency in the description, all of which speaks to greater confidence in our understanding.

- By contrast, people were less confident about describing how Kindness was experienced; possibly, we are worried about others judging us as unkind and doubt our ability to be the referee.

- People also indicated low confidence in evaluating others' Kindness, which may speak to the fragile ways that we express opinions and insult, without tending towards certain outcomes.

- When describing Kindness, we have a highly emotional and positive tone. When we move to how we have experienced it, we switch to an analytical tone, almost devoid of emotion, very clinical.

- People describe Kindness as the mortar or glue, language around building such states as trust and safety. Lots of words are used around building, growing and creating.

Kindness

QUIET LEADERSHIP

FAIRNESS
IN OUR ACTIONS

AS WE FIND STRENGTH

In the journey of Quiet Leadership, we reach maturity: The sapling is now a tree, with a canopy that reaches out wide.

In our formal leadership, we have found power, and with that power comes a choice: Do we use it for ourselves, or in service to others? Do we find reward or create shade and shelter?

As we grow strong,

As we find height and reach

As we gain power

Fairness

We can use it to reward ourself, or to reach out to shelter others.

©Julian Stodd

SEA SALT LEARNING

HOW DO WE EXPERIENCE FAIRNESS?

Our sense of fairness is finely tuned and emerges early in our development. At two years old, my son is acutely aware of what is fair, and what is not, although it is equally clear to me that his understanding of fairness is calibrated around himself.

If I am eating a slice of toast, he comes over to demand some and is upset if I do not share. But if I ask him for something that he holds, I am usually rewarded with a 'no'.

Whilst our strategies become more elaborate, our sense of fairness is deeply rooted and continues to influence or control our behaviour and response, throughout our lives.

We do not experience fairness in absolute terms so much as relative ones. If I do a job and am paid for

Fairness

SEA SALT LEARNING

it, I may not have a view on whether the reward is fair until I am aware of how much you were paid to do the same job.

If you are paid more for identical work, I am unlikely to believe my reward is fair.

And if you refuse to tell me how much you are paid, I may consider that you are acting unfairly too, as you are preventing me from knowing how I am being treated. As I said above: my understanding of fairness is calibrated around myself.

So fairness may be judged in relative terms but also, perhaps, abstractly. If something is demanded of me, I may simply decide, or feel, that it is unfair.

Similarly, when people become ill, are bereaved or experience the loss of love, they may want to shout about how unfair things are, even though none of us can seriously believe that we hold any intrinsic right to fairness from something as ethereal as the universe.

But what is the experience of fairness? Does it relate to the gain of something physical or tangible, or is it more a feeling or desire?

Whilst fairness is often expressed in terms of quantity or value (e.g. more cake, less money), it tends to be the relative amount rather than the currency itself that counts, and it may tend to be in relation to something else.

So the amount of cake I have may be fair or unfair, depending upon how much I paid, or how much you have.

The slice itself in isolation is intrinsically neither fair nor unfair.

We see this in a broader conversation about equity and equality: Equity is judged according to need, whilst equality is considered in absolute terms.

For example, I should probably consume around 2,500 calories a day. I may choose to buy organic bread, artisanal chocolate, and free-range eggs to do so.

Now imagine that you, as my friend, have lost your job, and are unable to feed yourself. I choose to buy your weekly groceries to support you, and I duly deliver tinned potatoes, rice and beans to your doorstep, with the calorific value of 2,500 calories per day.

I have delivered according to your need. We both have 2,500 calories, which may mean we have an equitable arrangement.

But we do not have an equal one by the standards of quality or taste (assuming you believe that my artisanal chocolate has some better quality to it).

But is it fair? Or unfair?

I guess I have acted fairly (or intended to do so) by gifting you the food.

Indeed, you may consider it fair too, whilst simultaneously believing that it is unfair that you are driven into this situation by society.

Some people moderate their actions with a system of beliefs that indicate an external moderation of fairness, be it by a deity or karma. They may say that I should share everything with you equally.

We seem to recognise, at least in more civilised parts of the world, that some things are common goods or rights, such as access to clean drinking water and protection by the police.

Here in the UK, the utility company cannot, by law, cut off your water supply if you cannot pay your bill. It would be unfair and a greater unfairness than the loss of revenue to the company.

Fairness is complex, often held in these nuanced and stacked arrangements, where the action is judged in context and subjectively.

QUESTION 5:

With fairness, where does our responsibility lie?

With Fairness Where Does Our Responsibility Lie?

We can become conflicted within systems. We owe a duty of care, as well as both contractual and legal responsibilities, in various directions, all held within our own moral and ethical frameworks.

If I am contracted to an Organisation, then my contract often defines the edges of this responsibility, for example, not to share commercially sensitive information outside the four walls.

So, I have clear legal responsibilities.

I also have moral ones. If I sign the contract, I have not only a legal responsibility to abide by the terms but also a moral one to keep my word, because an employment contract is also a commitment to the Organisation.

This second type of contract exists only in my head, perhaps; nonetheless, we are tightly governed by such imaginary constructs.

I also have other responsibilities. If we are trusted teammates or friends, we are held within social contracts, bonds of trust, bonds of shared experience and ties of shared challenge.

If you ask people what forms the dominant moderation of their actions, they typically respond that it is social ties that trump formal ones. Essentially I am more likely to abide by the rules out of my responsibility to you or fear of your judgement than because I fear formal sanction alone.

So, in your conversation, consider this: Where does your responsibility lie? What is your instinctive reaction, your emotional one, or your logical one?

And do they line up or sometimes split apart?

HOW FAIRNESS IS SPLIT

In the question, we asked where the tensions lie. As with any tension, if it increases, the thing in question may split.

So, how does fairness split and fail? What causes the branch to break?

What Splits Fairness?

Where Does The Tension Lie

Is it the act of discovery?

When I learn how much you are paid, is that the point at which my sense of fairness splits?

Or is an act unfair, even if undiscovered?

If you have to act unfairly but are not discovered, does your soul remain untarnished?

Is it the action that damages it, or the discovery?

And is unfairness itself sometimes fair?

In my previous example, I am feeding you tinned beans, despite being able to afford chocolate myself—an action that may be equitable but unequal and, possibly, fair or unfair, depending upon your perspective.

But what if I am using the money I save to achieve some other social good?

What if I spend half of my surplus income on you and the other half on a charity saving baby dolphins?

Where does the tension lie?

Is it the divide between you and Flipper or between my toasted rye ciabatta and your boiled potatoes, or somewhere else?

What if I chose to eat the same tinned beans as you, but gifted the better food to a food bank?

The tensions we feel may not be this abstract. What about at work? If I know you, am I likely to act more fairly towards you?

When it comes to negotiating opportunity, pay or formal recognition, am I more likely to favour you if I know and like you?

And what if the needs of the Organisation (to which I am legally tied and morally responsible) lie in direct contrast to your needs expressed by you (to whom I am tied by trust and community)?

If I know that you are at risk of redundancy, but I am not allowed to tell you at the very moment you are making a costly financial decision about a new car, should I tell you of the risk, or not?

Should I break my moral obligation to the contract in favour of my moral obligation to you?

And if I break the one I have to you, should I also break it to give Charlie such news too, even though I do not like Charlie?

These are, of course, all relative choices. The thing to take away is that Fairness is a fragile construct, strongly deterministic of our actions but, as we saw with Kindness, potentially unevenly distributed and complex in the execution.

Fairness

QUESTION 6:

Does your power promote growth?

Does your power promote growth?

Consider how you use your power. In the full majesty of the spreading canopy, do you use it to shelter, enable or what?

Consider, too, how that lands. Do people want the shelter you can give them?

Or does that speak of old power?

Use this question to explore how you use Fairness in your own leadership, or how you see it more broadly used in your Organisation.

SEA SALT LEARNING

REACHING DOWN

So much of our Organisational life is focused upwards: We climb ladders, get promoted and align both wealth and power with seniority. But what if the work of a Quiet Leader is to reach down?

A great deal of our Organisational design and structure is a legacy of our heritage of industrialisation, globalisation and capitalism, all of which carried us to where we are today. But what if they are not the whole of the answer?

What if leaders should let things go?

Every single day, reach down, to those earlier in their career, to those who are junior in the Organisation, to those just starting their journey.

And ask how you can help...

...through access to networking, through opportunity, through a listening ear or a helping hand...

...simply by demonstrating the humanity of a hierarchy.

Often, we see that it is easier (and more common) for people to network sideways and upwards, but by reaching down, you can benefit too, by becoming more interconnected...

...by hearing alternative realities that may be very different from your own, by hearing stories that are unfamiliar.

The degradation of our cultural ecosystems is a consequence of fragmentation. Hence, our every act of rebalancing, of connection, truly counts.

To Leave With Less

© Julian Stodd

LEAVING WITH LESS #1

One view of Fairness would be a more equitable division of opportunity, freedom, recognition and reward.

This is not simply about money; it's about the social currencies of belonging and belief.

We can each, through the smallest of actions, give more away.

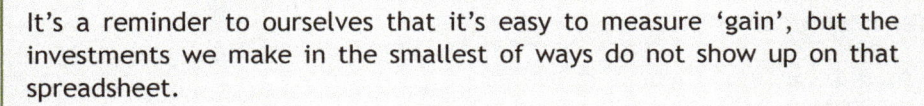

It's a reminder to ourselves that it's easy to measure 'gain', but the investments we make in the smallest of ways do not show up on that spreadsheet.

Leave with less by reaching out, by reaching down, by reaching beyond the light, by reaching beyond the walls—and give something.

Again, this may be about opportunity or resource, but it could just as well be about space to speak or an audience for the story.

So often we focus on how can get heard, to the point that we almost forget what it is to listen.

To leave with less is a commitment to others but also a gift to ourselves.

Recognise and remember that the prize does not come from what we carry to the finish line but, rather, in the nature of the journey by which we get there.

In the Ecosystem of the Organisation, to leave with less is to tread lightly through the landscape but to walk far and wide throughout it.

WHAT OUR RESEARCH SAYS ABOUT FAIRNESS

An initial reading of the Quiet Leadership research leads to the following narrative:

- We seem to feel a strong but not universal responsibility to be fair. We tend to leave ourselves some wriggle room.

- People are quite strongly ambiguous when responding to whether it is sometimes ok to be unfair.

- As with Kindness there is variability as to whether Fairness is held within our intent or our impact, although we tend to believe that the impact holds the judgement of others.

- When asked to whom we owe fairness, the most common answer (and contrary to apparent action) is 'everyone', closely followed by 'ourselves'. This tension between stating that Fairness should be owed equally to everyone, yet recognising (in Kindness, for example) that we spend it unevenly, is interesting and a core theme in Quiet Leadership.

- There is a strongly held view that it is important to be fair to the people whom we manage. This probably speaks volumes to the challenges of change that typically exists as an act of violence and loss to these very tribes.

- Highly analytical language tends to be used to describe what fairness is: a lot of conversation about the distribution of resources (e.g. attention, resources, knowledge, power), a strong sense of equity related to fairness.

- We live in a world that is not rational; fairness seems to support us through those dips and valleys.

- The third most popular thing stated, to which we 'owe' fairness, is 'the earth', which may be an interesting contemporary Dominant Narrative.

- We believe that Fairness is really important, but we also seem to retain some wriggle room for our personal operation. So, in that sense, universal fairness can be judged an abstract aspiration, whilst perhaps the more pragmatic aspects of life colour our actions.

Fairness

QUIET LEADERSHIP

GRACE
IN LETTING GO

THE BREEZE

Grace describes fluidity of action, a model of leadership that is adaptive, contextual and evolutionary. It's not about strength that is held rigidly but, rather, with fluidity.

It's an expression of leadership as a course correction, where we constantly monitor the way we sit in that ecosystem, making small changes but making them every day.

It is leadership as the breeze through the forest.

Quiet Leadership is about letting go; about relinquishing power or outdated beliefs, letting go of constraint, abandoning the abstractions of scale in favour of the grounded reality of our individual actions in this very moment.

Quiet Leadership is not a programme but, rather, our own performance.

Quiet Leadership is not about the gain of power or scale but, rather, about connection and meaning.

Quiet Leadership is not the end of a long journey but, rather, the first three steps.

Grace

WEATHERING THE WINTER STORMS

In the seasons of Quiet Leadership, we have seen the tree grow, from the winter snow and through the springtime showers, the majesty of the summer canopy and the shade that it casts.

Now, as autumn approaches, we see the trees lose their leaves.

Trees Lose Their Leaves To Weather The Winter Storms

We can all too easily see the autumn as a time of loss, before the ultimate darkness of the winter.

But what if we view it instead as part of the cycle? The autumn prepares us for winter, and from the winter comes the life of spring.

Trees lose their leaves in the winter, not as a process of death and decay but, rather, that they may weather the winter storms.

If they keep them, their branches may break with the weight of snow or fury of the storm.

Better instead to shed them actively—an act of wilful loss.

THE FOREST GROWS FROM THE FLOOR

Through the Autumn, the leaves form a thick carpet on the forest floor. In those months, as the nights close in, it is easy to view this as a lifeless, cold and damp place, but the truth is different.

Whilst we look up to see the glorious canopy, the greens fading to yellow, orange and rich reds, to see the sun, to reach for the light, the forest itself grows from the floor.

The leaves that we shed in the autumn form the most complex part of our ecosystems: the fungi and moulds, the insects and animals, these together create the leaf mould and soil.

And soils are some of the most complex systems that we know, almost impossible to create artificially; they are dynamic, living systems and structures.

The ecosystem cannot thrive if the trees hold their leaves; and the forest floor, whilst lacking beauty, is as much an aspect of beauty as the view overall.

In a systemic, ecosystem view, beauty is an emergent feature of the connected landscape, much as culture is an emergent feature of connected people.

AN ENDLESS WEIGHT

'Grace' is about a fluidity of style, a recognition that leadership is not something we are awarded or achieve, so much as a state within which we try to remain.

I chose the word as it's about graceful execution but also a quality of care and choreography.

Some years ago, in Singapore, I spoke to a choreographer about the written notation of dance. She described how the language conveyed the positioning of the body within a 3-D matrix that five dancers may interpret in five different ways in their performance.

The Grace of our Quiet Leadership is that individual aspect of our performance.

Consider the weight that we each carry. It's easy for us to focus on the noise, on the visible loads, but, of course, many people carry other weights that we cannot see.

They carry burdens of care, of their own mental health and well-being, of commitments to other communities, of vulnerability and self-doubt.

The only two things we can say for sure are that everyone carries weight, and nobody can carry an endless load.

Part of the grace in Quiet Leadership is to learn how to ask about that weight and be willing to bear heavy burdens together.

QUESTION 7:

What weight do you carry?

What Weight Do You Carry

For Yourself *For Others*

You can answer this however you like:

- The weight that you carry for yourself
- The weight that you carry for others
- A weight that everyone can see as they look at you
- A weight that is hidden from others but heavy nonetheless
- The weight that you see people carrying
- A weight that you need to put down

We do not have to know the details of every weight that people carry. On this journey, the important thing is not to ensure that everyone carries the same weight but, rather, to ensure that we carry what we are able, and nobody carries too much weight alone.

LEAVING WITH LESS #2

An act of Quiet Leadership is to seek to leave with less.

At the end of a day, when you have won, when you carry everything you need, then seek to give something away, to leave with less.

At the end of a day when you are losing, you feel exhausted, you have almost nothing left to give, use that last moment to leave with less.

You can give away:

- Resource - give someone something that they need

- Belief - give yourself permission to abandon a belief that no longer serves you well

- Connection - give someone a new connection or conversation

- Doubt - share a doubt, because you may create space for people to invest

- Uncertainty - share something about which you are unsure because, by doing so, you may create space for others to share their uncertainty and doubt, because we are all human

- Gratitude - leave the day with gratitude to others, reach out with thanks, shared within the context of what that person has given you

- Fear - leave behind a fear, not through exhaustion, but as a landmark that we have left in the distant past

- Power - use your power to shield, support, enable, or simply to create a rock to which people can cling—let them know

QUESTION 8:

What can you leave behind?

As the leaves fall from the tree, what will you put down, what can you leave behind?

Not something that has been taken from you, but something that may have served you well, but now the time is right to let it go.

Go into the Winter by willingly letting go, the better to have the strength you will need ahead.

WHAT OUR RESEARCH SAYS ABOUT GRACE

This is an initial narrative from the research:

- Nobody thought that Leadership was entirely effortless; most believed that it involved at least some course correction.

- Almost all respondents believed that Leadership could be described as an evolutionary process, one that never stops.

- Most people felt unable to evaluate whether they have a natural rhythm in their Leadership. Whilst they found it hard to evaluate it in themselves, they wrote a lot of words about it, which may represent questing for an answer through narrative.

- Most people believe that their Leadership practice is more reflective than reactive; they did not believe they were buffeted too badly by the storms.

- In general, people found it quite hard to articulate their own Leadership.

- People expressed their inability to act in harmony with their Organisation when they lacked the knowledge of intent, or when there was a misalignment of core values. This is unsurprising.

- There was strong agreement that feedback is necessary to ascertain our impact as a Leader.

- People strongly agreed that reflection is important for course correction.

- Trust was identified as a disrupter; the lack of it prevents us from acting in harmony with the Organisation. It was described as the 'oil'.

Grace

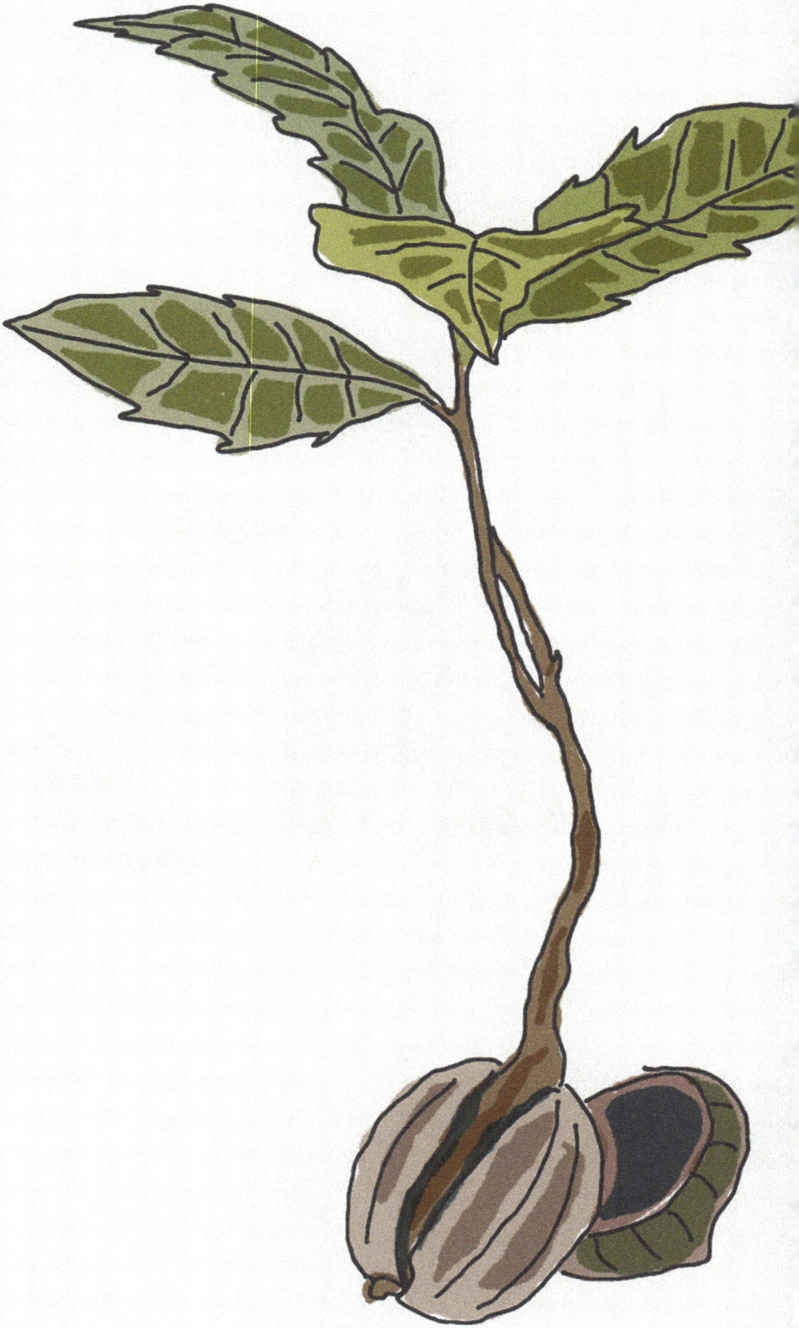

Quiet Leadership

IN PRACTICE

QUIET LEADERSHIP

The notion of Quiet Leadership is neither a formal programme nor something that you learn from a book. It is a journey, across a landscape, within an ecosystem, through four seasons.

1. Some ideas sit at the heart of this landscape:

- We each cast a shadow.

- Our systems are full of good people, but our shadows may intersect.

- Our intention is not the same as our impact.

- Social currencies are not necessarily evenly distributed.

- Power can be found as much in what you give away as in that which you hoard.

- Nobody can tend to the ecosystem alone... and yet, without our collective action, the ecosystem cannot be healthy.

I said at the start that if Organisations talk about change as a journey of 10,000 steps, then Quiet Leadership would be the first three.

We have made this journey based on eight questions, but really, you could have chosen any questions that you liked.

This book, this journey, is not one of answers, of 'right' or 'wrong' but, rather, one of reflection, and a recognition that what I think is 'right' is less important than my understanding of the ways that I am experienced within the ecosystem.

I am judged on my actions more than my intent, and that is as it should be.

The section on Grace represents the most recent part of my work on Quiet Leadership and, hence, perhaps the least well-formed.

But I believe that the intent is right: Leadership is not a destination that we reach, but a journey that we make.

And that it can be the smallest actions that truly count.

WALKING THROUGH THE FOREST

Every day, each of us, through the smallest of actions, takes something out of this system and puts something into it.

We all contribute and consume.

We enhance and degrade, through our every action.

Quiet Leadership is an active practice, in the arms of our Community.

Walk through the forest and see the beauty of the canopy, the interplay of light and shade, feel the rich earth under your feet.

Part of the journey is the intent: the starting point and the destination.

Part of the journey is the experience of being lost, of snatched glimpses through the trees, of emerging into the sunlight, onto the heath.

Without the eyes of others, we cannot see into our shadow. Cultivate your Communities and the bonds of trust that will enable you to hear what you need to hear.

You cannot tend to the ecosystem alone, but without your action, the ecosystem cannot thrive.

FURTHER READING

THE GUIDEBOOK SERIES

I've written a series of *'Guidebooks'* for the Social Age: these cover aspects of my work that are still rapidly evolving, or which I have not made time to write a full book about yet. They are typically under 10k words, and are intended to provide an overview of the landscape. I try to keep them practical, with a key highlight on *'what you need to know'*, and *'what you can do about it'*.

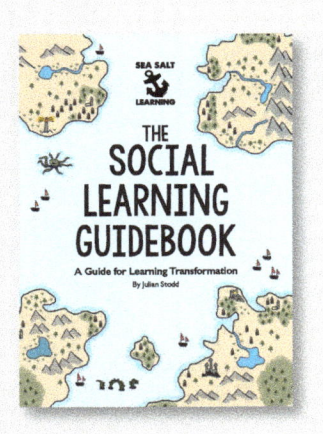

The Social Learning Guidebook provides a practical overview for the principles and design techniques of Social Learning in a modern organisation.

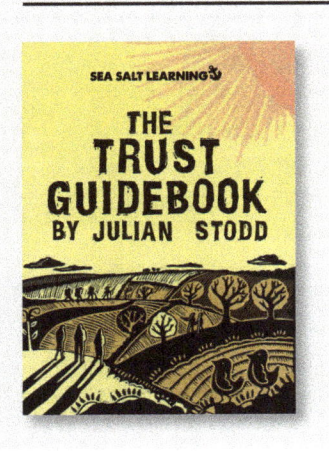

The Trust Guidebook explores our extensive research into the Landscape of Trust, and asks 72 questions that leaders can use with their teams.

Finding Your Campfire This short book is a survival guide for individuals, teams, and organisations navigating the experience of remote work.

The Humble Leader
The Humble Leader is a guided reflection into our personal humility as a Social Leader.

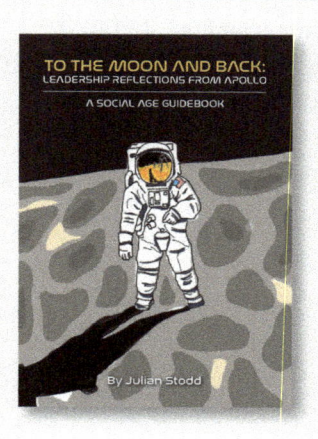

To the Moon and Back: Leadership Reflections from Apollo shares eight key stories about the Apollo programme, alongside my personal reflection on what this means for Leadership in the Social Age.

Further Reading

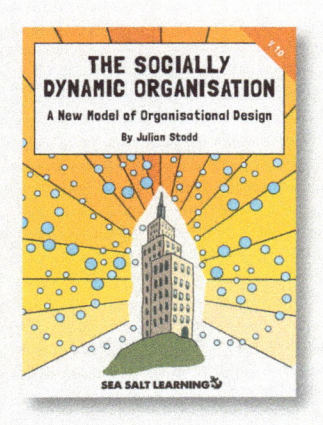

The Socially Dynamic Organisation
For a new type of world, we will need a new type of Organisation: one that is lightweight and rapidly adaptable, that thrives in times of constant change, that respects the old but embraces the new.

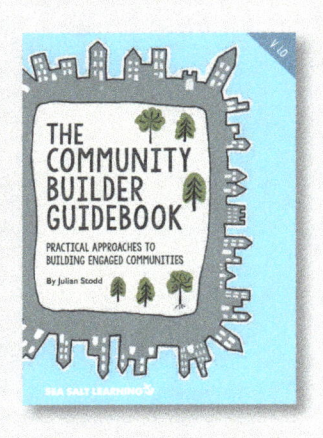

The Community Builder Guidebook brings you practical ideas to create engaged and dynamic Social Learning Communities and Communities of Practice.

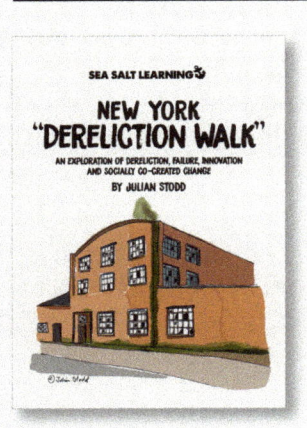

The New York Dereliction Walk is more experimental work, exploring how Organisations and ideas fall derelict and fail, but can be reborn through social movements. It was my favourite writing from 2018.

THE HANDBOOK SERIES

'Handbooks' are intended to capture a full snapshot of my evolving body of work on a particular subject. *'The Social Leadership Handbook'*, now in its second edition, explores the intersection of Formal and Social authority, and considers the importance of this in the context of the Social Age.

I'm currently finishing writing *'The Change Handbook'*, which is an exploration of how Organisations change, and the forces that hold them constrained. It considers how we build more Socially Dynamic Organisations.

Further Reading

THE '100 DAY', & 'SKETCHBOOK', SERIES

Whilst *'Handbooks'* and *'Guidebooks'* are about ideas and strategy, the *'100 Day'* books tackle how we do these things at scale. They do so by providing a scaffolded space, which you can explore, document, and graffiti, as you go.

'Social Leadership: My First 100 Days' is a practical, guided, reflective journey. It follows 100 days of activity, with each day including provocations, questions, and actions. You fill in the book as you go. It's accompanied by a full set of 100 podcasts.

'The Trust Sketchbook' is another guided, reflective journey, a walk through the Landscape of Trust, but in this case you graffiti and adapt the book, to capture your own landscape.

OTHER BOOKS

I have written a series of other books, covering aspects of learning, culture technology, and knowledge, which you can find details of on the blog.

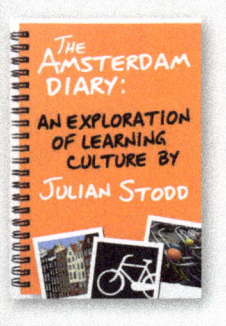

SEA SALT LEARNING   97

CERTIFICATIONS

In 2018 I launched the first Certification programme on *'Storytelling in Social Leadership'*. It's based upon *'Foundations'* and *'Techniques'*, which are practical and applied, and *'Experiments'*, which you learn to run in your own Organisation.

'Storytelling in Social Leadership'
'Leading with Trust'
'Community Building'
'Foundations of Social Leadership'

'Modern Learning Capabilities'
'Leading Through Change'
'Social Age Navigation'

Get in touch to find out more
www.seasaltlearning.com/certifications

MOOCS, PODCASTS, BLOGS & LOGS

Moocs and Podcasts

I run two MOOCs, one on 'Foundations of the Social Age', and one to accompany 'Social Leadership: My First 100 Days'.
You can find details at www.seasaltlearning.com, or drop me a line. I publish occasional podcasts, on all aspects of my work. You can find me through your usual podcast player.

The Blog and the Captains Log

I run two MOOCs, one on *'Foundations of the Social Age'*, and one to accompany *'Social Leadership: My First 100 Days'*. You can find details at seasaltlearning.com, or drop me a line.
I publish occasional podcasts, on all aspects of my work. You can find me through your usual podcast player.

Sea Salt Learning

In a more formal space, I founded Sea Salt Learning in 2014, acting as a global partner for change. We help some of the biggest and most interesting Organisations in the world get fit for the Social Age, through strategic consulting, building capability in teams, and building programmes to reach out at scale.

ABOUT SEA SALT LEARNING

We are a dynamic *Social Age startup:* living the values we speak. We are virtualised, global, inclusive, and agile. We are a core team of around twenty Crew Mates.

We are surrounded by a much larger layer of Social Age *'Explorers'*, people who are heavily involved in *'sense making'* around our core topics of Social Learning, Social Leadership, Change, Culture, and the Socially Dynamic Organisation.

Sea Salt Learning builds upon the work by Julian Stodd, author and explorer of the Social Age, recognised for his pioneering work in helping organisations to adapt to the new reality of the Social Age.

The *Sea Salt Research Hub* carries out original, creative, and large scale research, providing an evidence base for our work.

Sea Salt Publishing provides a curated body of books and online publications, exploring all aspects of the Social Age.

Sea Salt Digital provides our technical capability and build capacity for eLearning, mobile, video, and other forms of online learning.

Further Reading

SOCIAL AGE INSTITUTE

The Social Age Institute is a community for alumni and explorers of the Social Age: it is free and open for anyone to join.

I write a weekly newsletter for the group, as well as running regular open online sessions to share my latest research and work.

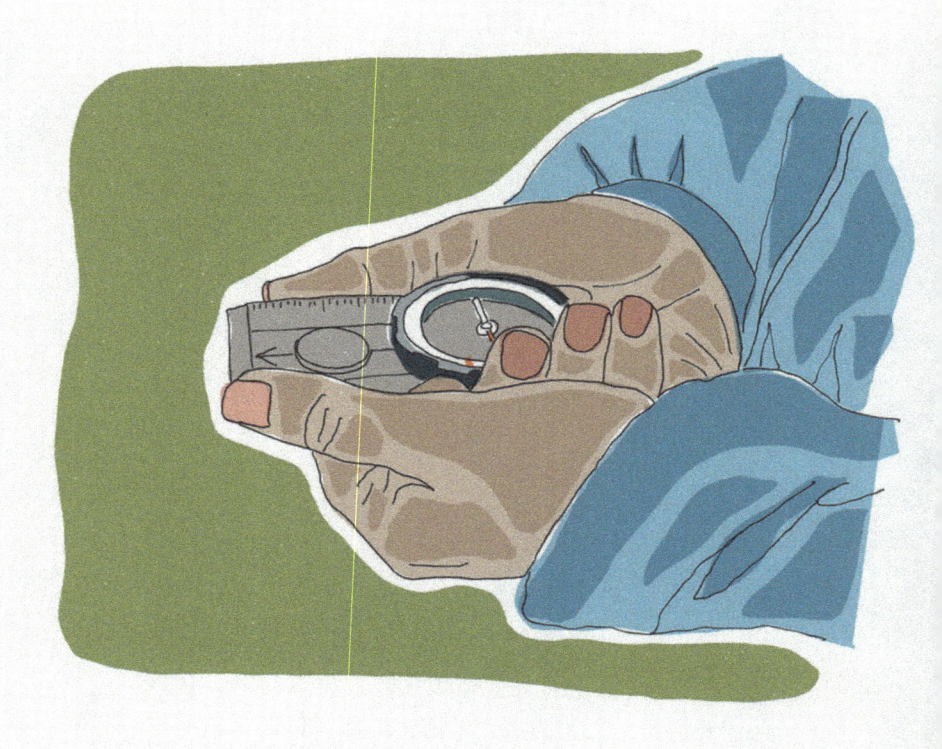

GETTING IN CONTACT

Find out more about how our Guidebooks can help you and your Organisation.

If you want to discuss any of the products in this Guidebook, or discuss your particular requirements, you can reach us here:

Talk to us: hello@seasaltlearning.com

Website: seasaltlearning.com

Find us on twitter: @seasaltlearning

Julian's blog: julianstodd.wordpress.com

Julian's twitter: @julianstodd

© Julian Stodd v1.0
09/2021

CPSIA information can be obtained
at www.ICGtesting.com
Printed in the USA
LVHW072345170922
728633LV00042B/1190

9 781838 019624